Prayer
PROMISES
for KIDS!

With Lots of Love
to Dia

From Nan

Cover and inside design by Chrystique Neibauer / Mellisa Hoffman, cqgraphicdesign.com
Cover design resources by www.shutterstock.com and Brenda's Kids

All Bible texts are from the New King James Version, copyright © 1979, 1980, 1982, Thomas Nelson, Inc., Publishers.

Additional copies of this book are available from two locations:
Adventist Book Centers: Call 1-800-765-6955 or visit http://www.adventistbookcenter.com
3ABN: Call 1-800-752-3226 or visit http://www.3abn.org

3ABN BOOKS is dedicated to bringing you the best in published materials consistent with the mission of Three Angels Broadcasting Network. Our goal is to uplift Jesus through books, audio, and video materials by our family of 3ABN presenters. Our in-depth Bible study guides, devotionals, biographies, and lifestyle materials promote the whole person in health and the mending of broken people. For more information, call 616-627-4651 or visit 3ABN's Web site: http://www.3abn.org.

Library of Congress Cataloging-in-Publication Data

Kuzma, Kay.
  Prayer promises for kids : more than 100 promises to pray, claim, and
believe / by Kay Kuzma and Brenda Walsh.
     p. cm.
  ISBN 13: 978-0-8163-2343-2 (paperback)
  ISBN 10: 0-8163-2343-7 (paperback)
  1. Christian children—Prayers and devotions. I. Walsh, Brenda, 1953-
II. Title.
  BV265.K89 2009
  242'.82—dc22

                                                                2009002975

09 10 11 12 13 • 5 4 3 2 1

Prayer PROMISES for KIDS!

3ABN BOOKS

Three Angels Broadcasting Network
West Frankfort, Illinois
www.3abn.org

Pacific Press® Publishing Association
Nampa, Idaho
Oshawa, Ontario, Canada
www.pacificpress.com

Kay Kuzma & Brenda Walsh

Prayer Topics

Prayer Topics

Prayer Topics

With Special Thanks

Kendra Adams	Kameron Hanna	Makayla Reynolds
Adrianna Bond	Psalmer Hermosa	Kylie Safford
Taylor Bond	Hannah Hoffman	Cameron Sanders
Pierce Burgess	Lance Hoffman	CJ Sanders
Taylor Canright	Mellisa Hoffman	Dionavin Sanders
Aaliah Carlos	Zana Hunt	Elizha Sanders
Anjali Chatlani	Zeayon Hunt	Joné Sanders
Alyssa Chung	Anne Jamieson	Jonesia Sanders
Justin Chung	Lee Jamieson	Stephanie Sanders
Michael Coffin	Jonny Kosaka	Jaslyn Sinclair
Sarah Devaraj	Timmy Kosaka	Noah Sinclair
Caleb Dinzey	Ben Krueger	Levi St. Clair
Samuel Dinzey	Katie Krueger	Dino Tsatalbasidis
Rosita Dvorak	Joshua Lance	Sofia Tsatalbasidis
James English	Judy Lance	Deanna Whitehouse
Selena English	Brandon Munson	Asher Wilson
Tyler English	Isabel Ong	Ashlee Wilson
Sonia Gott	Eliann Reinhardt	Sarah Wolfe

Dear Kids,

Prayer is the key that opens your heart to God. It's the way you say "Good Morning" to your best Friend, Jesus, and "Good Night" at the end of the day. It's the way you plug into Jesus' heavenly cell phone, because He is always there, always listening, and always ready with an answer to anything you might ask.

Jesus wants to be a part of your life. He wants to enjoy your family with you, go to school with you, play sports with you, take tests with you, ride in the car with you … and He wants to meet you each week in church.

Jesus has given you many promises in His Book, the Bible. He wants you to know what He has promised and He wants you to claim them for your own because He is eager to keep those promises.

Prayer isn't some series of words you memorize to make God listen to you. It's a conversation between you and God, and the prayers in this book are here to help you understand how REAL those conversations are. Don't simply pray *these* prayers but use them as ideas on how you can talk with your best Friend, Jesus!

This book will help you learn about Bible promises so you can ask Jesus for them. Maybe you have never prayed before or you want to learn a new way to pray. If so, there are more than one hundred sample prayers ready for you to pray. Why don't you talk to Him right now?

Kay Kuzma and Brenda Walsh

Accepting Others

Dear Jesus, sometimes I'm not very nice to other kids, especially when they look weird or talk funny or different. But I know You say in the Bible that I'm supposed to love everyone. I want to treat people the way that You want me to, so I claim Your promise in **Romans 15:7**, *"Therefore receive [accept] one another, just as Christ also received [accepted] us, to the glory of God."* Thank You for helping me be like You. **Amen**.

Afraid to be Alone

Dear Jesus, help me not to be afraid when I'm by myself. I claim Your promise in **John 14:27**, " 'Peace I leave with you, My peace I give to you; not as the world gives do I give to you. Let not your heart be troubled, neither let it be afraid.' " When I'm scared, help me to remember that I'm not really alone because You are always with me and will take care of me. Please help me to feel safe and trust You more. **Amen**.

Afraid of Bullies

Dear Jesus, there are some kids who are mean to me and I'm really scared. I don't know what to do because they are bigger and they say they will hurt me. Jesus, please help me. I claim **Isaiah 41:10**, where You promise me, " ' *"Fear not, for I am with you; be not dismayed, for I am your God. I will strengthen you, yes, I will help you, I will uphold you with My righteous right hand." ' "* Please come into their hearts so they won't want to hurt anyone anymore! And help me to trust You and not be afraid. **Amen.**

Afraid of the Dark

Dear Jesus, I'm afraid of the dark. I don't like it when I can't see. I know there aren't ghosts or wild animals around me, but I'm still scared. So Jesus I claim **Psalm 34:7**, *"The angel of the Lord encamps all around those who fear Him, and delivers them."* Thank You for giving me my own guardian angel and for all the other angels You say are around me, even though I can't see them. Help me to be brave and remember that I don't have to be afraid because You are always with me! **Amen**.

Afraid of the Devil

Dear Jesus, I know the devil is evil and mean. He wants to make me do things I shouldn't. He wants to make me do bad things. But You are much more powerful. Help me not to be afraid of the devil. I claim Your promise in **2 Thessalonians 3:3**, *"But the Lord is faithful, who will establish you and guard you from the evil one."* Thank You Jesus for protecting me and keeping me safe. **Amen**.

Afraid of Dying

Dear Jesus, I don't want to die. Help me to remember Your promise in **1 Thessalonians 4:16, 17** that You are going to come down from heaven with a shout and the trumpet of God, *"And the dead in Christ will rise first. Then we who are alive and remain shall be caught up together with them in the clouds to meet the Lord in the air. And thus we shall always be with the Lord."* It's not so scary to think of dying when I remember that it's something like sleeping, only when I wake up, I'll be going to heaven with my family to live with You forever. Thank You for that promise. **Amen**.

Afraid to Sleep

Dear Jesus, when I go to sleep, I get scared of all the bad things that could happen to me. I think of all kinds of terrible things and I get so frightened I don't even want to close my eyes. When I go to bed, please help me think of good things. And please help me not to dream scary dreams—just sweet dreams.

I claim Your promise in **Proverbs 3:24**, *"When you lie down, you will not be afraid; yes, you will lie down and your sleep will be sweet."*

Thank You Jesus for caring for me and protecting me so I don't have to be afraid. **Amen.**

Anger

Dear Jesus, I'm so angry inside. I feel like yelling and screaming, but I know it wouldn't solve anything. Please help me to control my anger so I don't hurt others—even though they may have hurt me. Every time I get angry, help me to remember the promise in **Proverbs 16:32**, *"He who is slow to anger is better than the mighty, and he who rules his spirit than he who takes a city."* Jesus, please take away my temper and let me be more like You. Thank You for hearing my prayer. **Amen**.

Arguing

Dear Jesus, I hate arguing. I don't like to hear my family or my friends argue. But before I know it, I'm right in the middle, saying things I shouldn't. I'm just as bad or worse than others. Please forgive me. You promised Moses in **Exodus 4:12**, *" 'I will be with your mouth and teach you what you shall say.' "* Jesus, You did that for Moses. Please do it for me too, so I won't argue and bicker with my family and my friends. Please teach me to say only kind things. **Amen**.

Attitude

Dear Jesus, my mom and dad say I have an attitude! I guess it's true. I don't want to be like this, but when things don't go my way, it makes me mad. I'm sure You didn't act this way when You were a kid, so I don't want to be this way either. But I've done it so much that it happens without me thinking. So Jesus please help me. I claim Your promise in **John 16:24**, *" 'Ask, and you will receive, that your joy may be full.' "* **Please** take away my bad attitude, and fill me with joy. **Amen**.

Bad Habits

Dear Jesus, I have a bad habit I can't seem to get rid of. I know what I'm doing isn't good for me, but I can't seem to stop myself. That's why I'm claiming Your promise in **Philippians 4:13** that *"I can do all things through Christ who strengthens me."* I can't do it alone. I need Your strength. Please come into my heart, and when I'm tempted, help me say No. With Your help, I know I can shake these bad habits. Thank You for helping me. **Amen**.

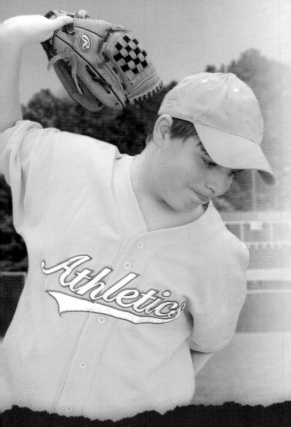

Bad Sport

Dear Jesus, please help me be a good sport. I don't know why, but I always want to win or be the best. When I lose, it makes me mad and I don't always act like I should. Sometimes I yell and scream and even throw things. I don't want to be this way anymore. I claim Your promise in **Proverbs 16:7**, *"When a man's [kid's] ways please the LORD, He makes even his enemies to be at peace with him."* I want my ways to please You too. Jesus, I really want to be a good sport, so help me to be happy for whoever wins. **Amen**.

Bad Temper

Dear Jesus, I have a bad temper and I need Your help! When I get frustrated or mad, without even thinking, I say and do things I don't really mean, and I want to change. With Your help, I'm claiming the promise in **Psalm 50:23**, " 'Whoever offers praise glorifies Me; and to him who orders his conduct aright I will show the salvation of God.' " I want to get rid of all these bad feelings inside me. When things go wrong, help me to praise You instead of losing my temper, because I want to go to heaven with You. Thank You Jesus for helping me. **Amen**.

Bedtime Prayer

Dear Jesus, thank You for being with me today. Forgive me for my sins and help me to be kind to others. Bless my family and friends. Help me to always keep You in my heart and be willing to share Your love wherever I go. Please send Your angels to watch over me while I sleep, like You say You'll do in **Psalm 91:11**, *"For He shall give His angels charge over you, to keep you in all your ways."* Please give me a good night's rest and help me to have sweet dreams. Thank You Jesus for loving me so much. **Amen**.

Bible Study

Dear Jesus, I want to grow closer to You and be more like You. I know I will grow more like You if I read my Bible. Help me to make time for You each day. I get so busy doing things I want to do that sometimes I forget to put You first! I love how You talk to me when I read Your Holy Word. That's why I'm claiming Your promise in **Psalm 119:11**, *"Your word I have hidden in my heart, that I might not sin against You."* I pray that You will help me study my Bible every day and memorize Your promises. I love You Jesus. **Amen**.

Bible Truth

Dear Jesus, I believe in the Bible and I believe everything You say is true. When others question what You say, help me to remember **Mark 13:31**, " *'Heaven and earth will pass away, but My words will by no means pass away.'* " Thank You for the Bible and all the stories that show me how much You love me. And please help me to read it more and memorize texts that will help me all my life. **Amen**.

Blessing for Meals

Dear Jesus, bless this food I'm about to eat and also the person who made it. Thank You for Your promise in **Matthew 6:25**, where You say, " *'Do not worry about your life, what you will eat or what you will drink.'* " I'm so glad You promised to always take care of me. Thank You for giving me this food and may it help me grow strong and healthy. Please bless the kids who don't have anything to eat. And help me to love You more. **Amen**.

Blessings From God

Dear Jesus, thank You for loving me and giving me so much—my mom and dad, my friends, my house, and food to eat. You are so good to me. You have promised in **Psalm 84:11**, *"The LORD will give grace and glory; no good thing will He withhold from those who walk uprightly [do what is right]."* I know this is true, and I want to walk uprightly. Please help me always to do what You want me to do! Thank You Jesus for all Your blessings. **Amen**.

Bragging

Dear Jesus, I don't like it when my friends brag about how great they are or all the stuff they have, but sometimes I do the same thing! Help me not to brag about myself. Instead Jesus help me to remember **Ephesians 2:8, 9**, *"For by grace you have been saved through faith, and that not of yourselves; it is the gift of God, not of works, lest anyone should boast."* Please help me to think of others and not myself! **Amen**.

Changing Behavior

Dear Jesus, I don't like how I've been acting. Please help me to change my bad behavior. I'm so ashamed of myself. I want to change, I really do, but I know I can't do it by myself. That's why I claim **2 Corinthians 5:17**, *"Therefore, if anyone is in Christ, he is a new creation; old things have passed away; behold, all things have become new."* Jesus, I want to be a new person. Please come into my heart so I can be the person You want me to be. **Amen**.

Cheating

Dear Jesus, I know I shouldn't cheat, but sometimes I do it anyway. Afterwards, I always feel bad. Please forgive me. I don't want to be a cheater! When I'm tempted, I want to be strong like Daniel and do what is right. Help me to remember Your promise in **Philippians 4:19**, *"And my God shall supply all your need."* Help me to remember that I don't have to cheat because You will give me what I need! Help me to always be honest, even if that means losing a game or getting a bad grade! Most of all, help me to be more like You. **Amen**.

Choices

Dear Jesus, I don't know what I should do. I've made so many mistakes and bad things have happened. This time I want to do things right. I'm not smart enough to know the answer. I need You to guide me. I need Your wisdom to tell me what to do. That's why I'm claiming Your promise in **James 1:5**, *"If any of you lacks wisdom, let him ask of God, who gives to all liberally and without reproach, and it will be given to him."* Thank You for helping me make a good decision. **Amen**.

Comfort

Dear Jesus, I'm very sad. You know I've been crying and feeling sorry for myself. I really, really need You to tell me everything is going to be OK. So I'm claiming Your promise in **Jeremiah 31:13**, where You say, " *'For I will turn their mourning to joy, will comfort them, and make them rejoice rather than sorrow.'* " Thank You for promising that this sadness won't last forever, and that You'll put happiness back into my heart. **Amen**.

Comparing

Dear Jesus, when I compare myself to my friends, I feel so bad. It seems I'm always looking to see who is better than I am. Thank You for Your promise in **Galatians 6:4, 5**, *"But let each one examine his own work, and then he will have rejoicing in himself alone, and not in another. For each one shall bear his own load."* Help me to do my best and be happy with who I am, instead of being miserable because I'm not like someone else. **Amen**.

Complaining

Dear Jesus, I really need Your help! When things don't work out like I want, I complain. I know I should be happy with what I have, but instead I blame others and make them miserable when I'm miserable. I really like the Bible text, **Proverbs 12:25**, which says, *"Anxiety in the heart of man [kids] causes depression, but a good word makes it glad."* Instead of complaining and making others and myself all upset, help me to say nice things and make everyone glad. I'm claiming Your promise today. Thank You for making me a better person. **Amen**.

Confused

Dear God, I'm so confused and I need You to make things clear to me. But I don't even know what I should ask for. All I know is what Jesus said about You in **Matthew 6:8**, " *'For your Father knows the things you have need of before you ask Him.'* " What an awesome promise! You already know what I need. I claim that promise for myself! Please dear Jesus give me wisdom like You gave to King Solomon! Help me to make the right decision. I'm so glad I can trust You with my life. **Amen**.

Courage

Dear Jesus, sometimes I don't want to do stuff because I'm scared. I don't know what's going to happen and I don't want kids to make fun of me. What if I can't do what people expect me to do? What if I make a mistake? I need courage to stand up and do what is right, even though others don't. That's why I claim Your promise in **Psalm 31:24**, *"Be of good courage, and He shall strengthen your heart, all you who hope in the Lord."* Thank You for making me brave so I don't have to be afraid. **Amen**.

Criticism

Dear Jesus, I don't like it when people criticize me. And yet, I do it to others. I judge their motives and I notice bad things much quicker than the good things. I know my critical words have hurt my friends— and turned some into enemies. I want to change. I'm claiming **Luke 6:35**, where You say, " *'But love your enemies, do good . . . and your reward will be great, and you will be sons of the Most High. For He is kind to the unthankful and evil.'* " I want to be like You. Help me to be kind and see the good in others. Thank You Jesus for loving me. **Amen**.

Discouraged

Dear Jesus, I'm having a really bad day! I'm so discouraged. Why try? I work hard, do my best, and no one seems to care. Why do others always get rewarded and I get nothing? I feel like giving up. That's why I'm claiming the promise You made in **Galatians 6:9**, *"Let us not grow weary while doing good, for in due season we shall reap if we do not lose heart."* Lord, please don't let me lose heart. Help me to keep doing my best, even though it doesn't seem to make any difference. Thank You for promising that someday I'll be rewarded! **Amen**.

Divorce of Parents

Dear Jesus, my parents are getting a divorce and I'm so sad I just want to cry. I love my mom and dad. I don't want them to split up. What will happen to me? I want my family to be happy together, but I can't fix things. So Jesus please help us. I claim Your promise in **Psalm 34:18**, *"The LORD is near to those who have a broken heart, and saves such as have a contrite [humble] spirit."* Please Jesus save my family, and thank You for the promise that You will never leave me. **Amen**.

Doubt

Dear God, I'm really struggling with believing that You are real and that You really do keep Your promises. I want to believe, but sometimes I wonder if You are really there. Please help me to claim Your promise in **Isaiah 46:11**, where You say, *" 'I have spoken it; I will also bring it to pass.' "* When I think of all the promises You kept for others, I know You will do the same for me. Please forgive me for doubting You and help me always to remember that if You say it, You'll do it. **Amen**.

Eating Disorders

Dear Jesus, I really need Your help. I am struggling with a lot of food issues right now, and I just can't seem to win the battle. People say I'm too thin but when I look in a mirror, I look really fat. I hate who I am and what I look like! I know this is a disease but I can't get well without Your help! That's why I'm claiming **John 11:22**,

" 'But even now I know that whatever You ask of God, God will give You.' "

I'm asking You dear Jesus to save me! I know that if You can raise Lazarus from the dead, You can certainly take away my eating disorder. Thank You for loving me, even when I can't love myself. **Amen**.

Embarrassed

Dear Jesus, I get embarrassed when I have to be up front. It's even worse when kids make fun of me—or when adults laugh at me for some mistake. I just want to run and hide. In Psalm 22, it says they did the same thing to You. I claim Your promise in **Psalm 22:19**, *"But You, O Lord, do not be far from Me; O My Strength, hasten to help Me!"* Thank You for letting me know that when I'm embarrassed, You are near and will help me. **Amen**.

Failure

Dear Jesus, I just can't seem to do anything right. I want to do a good job at whatever I do, but I'm afraid that I won't be good enough. I feel like a failure when I make mistakes. I claim Your promise in **Psalm 91:15**, *"He shall call upon Me, and I will answer him; I will be with him in trouble; I will deliver him and honor him."* Help me not to make a fool of myself by doing something dumb, and help me not to worry about what others think of me because what You think is what really matters! Thank You Jesus for helping me to do my best. **Amen**.

Faith

Dear Jesus, sometimes my faith isn't very strong. I pray for things and nothing seems to happen. But I know that's because I can't see what You see. Help me to trust You more, because You know everything and You only want good things for me! I claim **Matthew 21:22**, where You promise, *" 'And whatever things you ask in prayer, believing, you will receive.' "* Thank You for answering my prayer according to Your will and what is best for me. Please help me to be patient and have more faith. **Amen**.

Fairness

Dear Jesus, You are a just God. You don't play favorites. I know You want us to be the same way. But something has happened that doesn't seem fair to me. What should I do? Should I speak up? Or should I just let it go? I know You say in **Proverbs 31:8, 9** that we are to speak up for those who cannot speak for themselves. Does that mean I should defend myself? Make Your will plain to me. I'm claiming Your promise in **Isaiah 30:18,** *"For the LORD is a God of justice; blessed are all those who wait for Him."* I trust You to work it all out. **Amen.**

Falsely Accused

Dear Jesus, kids are saying things about me that aren't true. I feel like telling them off! I know people said things about You that weren't true but You didn't get back at them. I want to be like You! That's why I claim Your promise in **Matthew 5:11, 12,** " *'Blessed are you when they revile and persecute you, and say all kinds of evil against you falsely.'* " Help me to remember I'm special and that I belong to You regardless of what people say. **Amen**.

Family

Dear Jesus, I'm so thankful for my family. I love them so much and I want us to be happy. Here's the promise I'm claiming for us in **Ephesians 5:2**, *"And walk in love, [esteeming and delighting in one another] as Christ also has loved us and given Himself for us, an offering and a sacrifice to God for a sweet-smelling aroma."* I want that so much. Please Jesus help us not to argue and put each other down. Please live in our home—and in our hearts—so that we will be like You. **Amen**.

Fighting

Dear Jesus, I know I shouldn't fight with others, but when someone challenges me, that is what I feel like doing. I know in my heart that's not what You would do! So Lord I claim Your promise in **1 Samuel 12:23** when You say, *"I will teach you the good and the right way.'"* Whenever I feel like fighting, instead of hauling off and hitting someone, or even thinking about it, help me to pray that You will teach me a better way. I know You won't let me down. **Amen**.

Forgiving Others

Dear Jesus, You know what happened to me wasn't fair, and I want to get even. The last thing I feel like doing is forgiving. But then I think of what people did to You Jesus and You forgave them. As hard as it is, I know I must forgive, because I've done things that were wrong and I need Your forgiveness. That's why I'm claiming Your promise in **Luke 6:37**, " *'Forgive, and you will be forgiven.'* " I want to be like You. Please give me forgiveness in my heart for everyone who has hurt me! Thank You Jesus. **Amen**.

Friends—Choosing the Right Ones

Dear Jesus, I really want Christian friends but my problem is I'm having a hard time finding good kids who will be my friends. In **John 14:14**, You have promised, *" 'If you ask anything in My name, I will do it.' "* So I am claiming that promise and asking You Jesus to please help me find at least one good friend. I would love to have a friend who loves You like I do. Thank You Jesus for hearing and answering my prayer. **Amen**.

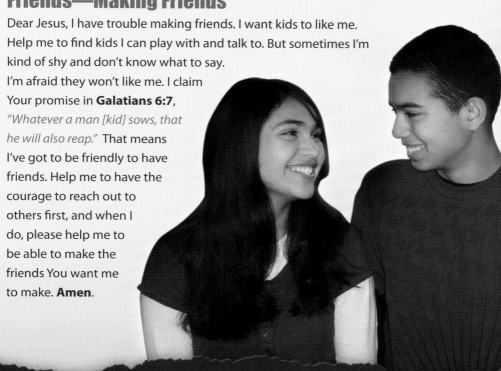

Friends—Making Friends

Dear Jesus, I have trouble making friends. I want kids to like me. Help me to find kids I can play with and talk to. But sometimes I'm kind of shy and don't know what to say. I'm afraid they won't like me. I claim Your promise in **Galatians 6:7**, *"Whatever a man [kid] sows, that he will also reap."* That means I've got to be friendly to have friends. Help me to have the courage to reach out to others first, and when I do, please help me to be able to make the friends You want me to make. **Amen**.

Friendship With Jesus

Dear Jesus, You are my best Friend. Some of my friends aren't very kind to me. Some don't even talk to me anymore. But I know You're not like that. You will always be kind and will never leave me. Thank You for being such a good Friend. Your promise really means a lot to me in **Isaiah 54:10**, " *'For the mountains shall depart and the hills be removed, but My kindness shall not depart from you.'* " Thank You for loving me so much. **Amen**.

Good Morning Prayer

Good morning, Jesus. Thank You for a good night's sleep. Help me to be good and obey my parents and be kind to others. You say in **Jeremiah 29:11**, *"For I know the thoughts [and plans] that I think toward you, says the LORD, thoughts of peace and not of evil, to give you a future and a hope."* I'm so glad I am always on Your mind. I give my heart to You Jesus because I love You so much. Thank You for all You do for me. Help me to be a good witness for You and let me tell someone today just how much You love them. I can't wait to see what You have planned for me. **Amen**.

Gossiping

Dear Jesus, people are saying things about me that aren't true. I don't know what to do. No one listens to me when I try to defend myself. So I'm claiming Your promise in **Job 5:21**, " *'You shall be hidden from the scourge of the tongue.'* " Thank You for protecting me. Please help me never to gossip about others because I've learned the hard way how much it hurts. Help me to only say kind things. Thank You for always taking care of me. I love You so much. **Amen**.

Guilty Feelings

Dear Jesus, I did something really, really bad. Even though I said I was sorry, my guilty conscience won't let me forget what I did. I don't like these guilty feelings. Please take them away. I've learned my lesson and with Your help, I won't do it again. I claim Your promise in **1 John 1:9**, *"If we confess our sins, He is faithful and just to forgive us our sins and to cleanse us from all unrighteousness."* Wash away my sin and my guilty feelings as You said You would do. Thank You Jesus. I feel better already. **Amen**.

Happiness

Dear Jesus, please give me a happy heart. I've been so sad that only You can make me happy again. You can turn bad things into good things. I'm claiming **Proverbs 16:20**, where You say, *"Whoever trusts in the LORD, happy is he."* I trust You Jesus. You know what's best for me. When I get sad, help me to think of You and all the good things You have planned for me. Thank You for turning my sad heart into a happy one. **Amen**.

Healing

Dear Jesus, my friend is sick and is hurting so much. Please help the pain to go away and help her/him to get well. It makes me sad to think about how much he/she is suffering. I claim Your promise in **Jeremiah 30:17**, where You say, " ' *"For I will restore health to you and heal you of your wounds."* ' " Jesus, I know You are better than any doctor and You love him/her even more than I do, so please heal him/her if it be Your will. Thank You for hearing and answering my prayer. **Amen**.

Heaven

Dear Jesus, I really want to go to heaven, but I know I don't deserve it. Sometimes I do things I shouldn't do, so I know I could never be good enough to get to heaven by myself. That's why I'm claiming Your promise in **John 3:16**, " *'For God so loved the world that He gave His only begotten Son, that whoever believes in Him should not perish but have everlasting life.'* " Thank You for loving me so much You died for me. I want to live in heaven with You forever. **Amen**.

Homework

Dear Jesus, I don't feel like doing my homework. I'm tempted to skip the hard parts and just turn in a half-done messy paper—just to get rid of it. But then I remember what You said in **Proverbs 22:29**, *"Do you see a man [kid] who excels in his work? He will stand before kings; he will not stand before unknown men."* I claim Your promise, that if I work hard and do my best, I'll someday stand before kings and well-known people. So help me to do my best on this homework assignment, even though I don't feel like it. **Amen**.

Honesty

Dear Jesus, I want to be honest and I want people to trust me, but sometimes I'm tempted to think it really doesn't matter if I'm honest or not, as long as no one gets hurt. It's easy to make excuses but inside I know that it's wrong to be dishonest. I claim Your promise in **Psalm 32:2**, *"Blessed is the man [kid] . . . in whose spirit there is no deceit."* Jesus, I want to be like that. I don't want to have any deceit in my life! Please help me always to be truthful. Help me to be more like You. **Amen**.

Hope

Dear Jesus, I am so very, very sad.
I don't feel like doing anything. I'm
feeling like King David in **Psalm 38:6**,
when he said he was troubled, bowed
down, and mourning all day long.
Help me Jesus to claim David's prayer
in **Psalm 38:15**, *"For in You, O LORD, I
hope; You will hear, O Lord my God."*
Please take away these sad feelings.
Hear my cry and put hope and joy
in my heart. Thank You. **Amen**.

Jealousy

Dear Jesus, sometimes I'm jealous when others have more than I do. Help me to be satisfied with the things I have instead of always wanting the things my friends have. That's why I'm claiming Your promise in **Proverbs 14:30**, *"A sound [calm] heart is life to the body, but envy [jealousy] is rottenness to the bones."* I don't want rotten bones! I don't want jealousy to make me sick. Instead, please help me to be thankful for all the things You have given me. **Amen**.

Kindness

Dear Jesus, when You lived on this earth You were kind to everyone—even to those who were mean to You. I want to be like You. Sometimes kids are mean to me and I feel like being mean to them and telling them off. Instead, please help me to be kind. Help me to treat everyone like I want to be treated, like the golden rule says in **Matthew 7:12**.
I know this is the right thing to do. I claim Your promise in **Proverbs 12:28**,
"In the way of righteousness [doing right] is life."
Thank You Jesus.
Amen.

Lazy

Dear Jesus, sometimes I'm lazy and don't want to do my homework or chores. I would rather lie around and watch TV, play video games, or text my friends. Help me not to be lazy. I claim Your promise in **Proverbs 28:19**, *"He who tills his land will have plenty of bread, but he who follows frivolity [wastes time] will have poverty enough!"* When I'd like to lie around but there is work to do, help me to make a good choice and do the work first. I don't want to end up poor because I'm too lazy to work. **Amen**.

Leader

Dear Jesus, I want to be a good leader. It's not that I just want to tell people what to do. I really want to be someone who will lead others to love You. I claim Your promise in **Deuteronomy 28:13**, *" 'And the LORD will make you the head and not the tail; you shall be above only, and not be beneath, if you heed the commandments of the LORD your God, which I command you today, and are careful to observe them.' "* Jesus, please help me to keep Your commandments so I can be a successful leader for You. **Amen**.

Learning

Dear Jesus, I'm having trouble remembering things I need to learn for a test. I don't like tests, especially when I don't know all the answers. I'm afraid I might flunk. I wish I was smarter. But Jesus, I know You know all the answers. Please help me remember what I have learned. I'm claiming Your promise in **Psalm 32:8**, where You say, *"I will instruct you and teach you in the way you should go; I will guide you with My eye."* When I'm not sure about an answer, please bring to my mind what I have studied. Thank You so much for helping me. **Amen**.

Living With Jesus

Dear Jesus, thank You for promising me that I can live with You forever. When I feel no one really cares about me, I repeat what You said in **John 14:2**, **3**, " *'In My Father's house are many mansions; if it were not so, I would have told you. I go to prepare a place for you. And if I go and prepare a place for you, I will come again and receive you to Myself; that where I am, there you may be also.'* "

It makes me feel special to know You're doing all this for me. Thank You.

Amen.

Lonely

Dear Jesus, I don't have anyone to hang out with or talk to and I feel so alone. Even my family is too busy to spend time with me. I'm so lonely I'm beginning to feel sorry for myself. But I'm thankful that I can always talk to You. I claim Your promise in **Hebrews 13:5**, " *'I will never leave you nor forsake you.'* " Thank You for being such a good Friend and for letting me know that I am really never alone, because You are always with me! You are such a cool and awesome God! I love You Jesus. **Amen**.

Lost Object

Dear Jesus, You know I have lost something I really need to find. I've looked everywhere and I don't know where it is. Please Jesus help me. You say in **Matthew 17:20**, that

" 'If you have faith as a mustard seed, you will say to this mountain, "Move from here to there," and it will move; and nothing will be impossible for you.' "

Jesus, I don't need the mountain to move, but I sure do need You to help me find what I lost. I believe You when You say that nothing is impossible with You. Thank You for helping me. **Amen**.

Love

Dear Jesus, I love my family and my friends, but sometimes I don't show it. In fact, I'm not feeling very loving right now. The way they treat me makes me angry and I say things I shouldn't. Please help me to be more like You. I claim Your promise in **1 John 4:12**, *"If we love one another, God abides in us, and His love has been perfected in us."* I'm asking You to live in my heart, so even if I don't feel very loving, I can show Your perfect love to others. I love You Jesus. **Amen**.

Loyalty

Dear Jesus, help me to stick up for my friends and family. Help me to be loyal. Help me to be strong when others are putting people down. I want to be like You. In **2 Chronicles 16:9**, it says, *" 'For the eyes of the LORD run to and fro throughout the whole earth, to show Himself strong on behalf of those whose heart is loyal to Him.' "* Thank You Jesus for being loyal to me. **Amen**.

Lying

Dear Jesus, sometimes I lie, and I don't know why I do it. Most are little "white lies," but they're still lies and I know it is a sin. I've tried to change on my own, but I keep messing up! That's why I claim Your promise in **Mark 10:27**, where You say, *" 'With men [kids] it is impossible, but not with God; for with God all things are possible.' "* I believe that with You, all things are possible, for You have the power to help people change. Please change me and give me the power to tell the truth! Thank You Jesus for helping me to break the habit of lying. **Amen**.

Money

Dear Jesus, I wish I had more money. I don't want to be greedy, but there are things that I'd like to buy—and my parents aren't exactly rich. In fact, sometimes I'm sure they worry about having enough money for our family. But You promise to supply all our needs. I want to claim **Psalm 34:10**, *"But those who seek the Lord shall not lack any good thing."* Every time I want something I really don't need, help me to remember this promise. And help me to give some money to help others learn about You, instead of just spending it on myself. **Amen**.

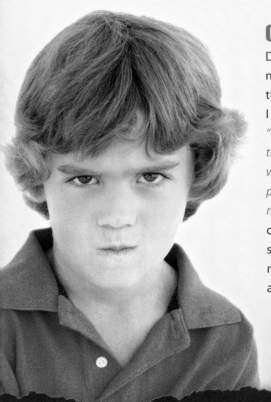

Obeying Parents

Dear Jesus, sometimes my parents make me angry and I don't feel like obeying them. But I know that wouldn't be right. I claim Your promise in **Ephesians 6:1–3**, *"Children, obey your parents in the Lord, for this is right. 'Honor your father and mother,' which is the first commandment with promise: 'that it may be well with you and you may live long on the earth.'"* Lord, I know I can't keep this commandment by myself, so every time I start to get mad, please give me the right attitude! Please help me to always be respectful and obedient. **Amen**.

Overeating

Dear Jesus, I just don't seem to be able to control my appetite. When I want something, I eat it. Sometimes when food tastes really good, I eat the whole thing. No matter how hard I try, I can't seem to stop! That's why I claim Your promise in **1 John 5:15**, *"That . . . whatever we ask, we know that we have the petitions that we have asked of Him."* Please help me to eat only food that is good for me, and don't let me stuff myself. Thank You Jesus for answering my prayer. **Amen**.

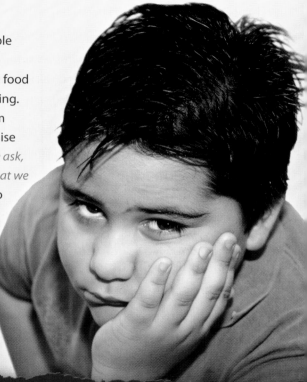

Patience

Dear Jesus, it's really tough for me to wait for things. I know I should be patient, but when I want something, I want it now. Even when I pray and ask for things, it's so hard for me to wait. So I want to claim the promise in **Psalm 37:34**, *"Wait on the LORD, and keep His way, and He shall exalt you to inherit the land."* That's a pretty big promise. Help me to learn patience. Help me to not get upset when things don't work out right away. Instead, help me to wait patiently for You to work things out. **Amen**.

Pets—Lost

Dear Jesus, my pet ran away and I can't find him. I've done everything I can think of. I've called the police, put up posters, and called for him all over the neighborhood, but he's lost! I'm so afraid something bad has happened. I love my pet so much, so please help us to find him or have him come home. I claim Your promise in **John 16:23**, *" 'Most assuredly, I say to you, whatever you ask the Father in My name He will give you.' "* Please Father, if it be Your will, I am asking in Jesus' name that my prayer be answered and my pet will come home. **Amen**.

Pets—Sick

Dear Jesus, I am so sad because my pet is sick and I'm so afraid he will die. I love him so much and I know You do too because You made all the animals. I claim Your promise for my pet in **Psalm 30:2**, *"O LORD my God, I cried out to You, and You healed me."* I believe that You have the power to heal and if it is Your will, please work a miracle and heal my pet. Thank You Jesus for hearing and answering my prayer. **Amen**.

Praising God

Dear Jesus, You are so good to me and have given me so much. I want to praise You with the words of **Psalm 103:2–4**, *"Bless the Lord, O my soul, and forget not all His benefits: who forgives all your iniquities, who heals all your diseases, who redeems your life from destruction, who crowns you with loving-kindness and tender mercies."* Help me never to forget how wonderful You are. **Amen**.

Prayer

Dear Jesus, I'm so glad I can pray to You any time and anywhere I want. Help me to remember to talk to You not just when I'm in trouble or when I want something, but help me to pray for others too. You are so awesome and I want to thank You for always being there for me! I claim Your promise in **Proverbs 15:8**, *"The sacrifice of the wicked is an abomination to the LORD, but the prayer of the upright is His delight."* Please keep me "upright" because I want to please You too! Thank You for hearing and answering my prayers, and for being my best Friend. I love You so much. **Amen**.

Pride

Dear Jesus, I think about myself a lot. I know I'm smart and talented and I can do many things better than others. But I don't want to be proud and conceited. I claim Your promise in **Luke 14:11**, " *'For whoever exalts himself will be humbled, and he who humbles himself will be exalted.'* " I know when I talk about myself, others don't like it—and I'm humbled! Help me to take You at Your word that if I'm humble, in Your time I will be "exalted." Help me to think more highly of others instead of myself. **Amen**.

Protection

Dear Jesus, I'm scared something bad is going to happen. Please keep me safe from harm and danger. Help me to remember Your promises in **Psalm 91**. I especially claim verses **3** and **4**; *"Surely He shall deliver you from the snare of the fowler [hidden traps] and from the perilous pestilence [deadly diseases]. He shall cover you with His feathers, and under His wings you shall take refuge; His truth shall be your shield and buckler [protection]."* It helps me to be brave knowing that You are always there for me. Thank You for protecting me. **Amen**.

Prayer Promises for Kids!

Punishment

Dear Jesus, I don't like it when I'm punished. I know my parents and teachers are trying to teach me to do what is right. Help me to not get mad when I'm punished and help me to learn from the mistakes I make. I claim Your promise in **Proverbs 13:18**, *"Poverty and shame will come to him who distains correction, but he who regards a rebuke will be honored."* Thank You for the promise that if I accept correction, I'll be honored. Please help me to make better choices so I won't have to be punished. **Amen**.

Rebellion

Dear Jesus, I feel like rebelling. I hate all the rules. I can't do anything I want to. My parents and teachers say I have a behavior problem. But I just want to do my own thing. It's like I have the devil inside me. He rebelled against You God, and he's pushing me to rebel too. But I really don't want to be like that. I want Satan out of my life. I want to be obedient. So I'm claiming **James 4:7**, *"Resist the devil and he will flee from you."* Jesus, please help me kick Satan out of my life. Thank You for answering my prayer. **Amen**.

Rejection

Dear Jesus, kids don't like me. I want to have friends. I want to be part of the in-group, but they push me away and say bad things about me. I don't know what to do to be accepted. Please help me. I claim Your promise in **Deuteronomy 20:4**, " ' "*For the* L*ORD* *your God is He who goes with you, to fight for you against your enemies, to save you.*" ' " Thank You for loving me and for fighting my battles for me so I don't have to. **Amen**.

Reputation

Dear Jesus, I want people to like me and to say nice things about me, but more importantly, I want to be like You. I know that won't happen unless I do what I should and avoid doing bad things. I claim **Proverbs 27:21**, *"The refining pot is for silver and the furnace for gold, and a man is valued by what others say of him."* Help me protect my reputation by doing what is right and living the way You want me to. In Your name I pray, **Amen**.

Rules

Dear Jesus, rules, rules, rules. I get so sick of all the rules! But then I remember Your promise in **John 13:17**, *" 'If you know these things, blessed [happy] are you if you do them.' "* I know it's true. Even though sometimes I feel like rebelling against rules that don't make sense, I always find that if I just keep them, I end up a whole lot happier because I don't get into trouble! Jesus, help me to respect and obey the rules of my parents, school, government, and most importantly, Your rules too. **Amen**.

Sabbath

Dear Jesus, help me to love the Sabbath and enjoy worshiping You. Sometimes I forget how special Your day is and I just want it to be over with so I can do my own thing. But I know that's not right and I don't want to miss Your special blessing You promise in **Isaiah 56:2**, " *'Blessed is the man [kid] . . . who keeps from defiling the Sabbath, and keeps his hand from doing any evil.'* " Help me to only do good things on Your Sabbath day, and please help me to love the Sabbath so much that I'm always looking forward to spending this special day with You. **Amen**.

Safe Travel

Dear Jesus, please be with me as I travel today and keep me safe from accidents. I pray Lord that my guardian angel will be with me at all times. I claim Your promise in **Psalm 85:13**, *"Righteousness will go before Him, and shall make His footsteps our pathway."* Thank You for going before me and keeping me safe. Please help me to be a good witness to everyone I meet today. **Amen.**

Saved

Dear Jesus, thank You for loving me so much that You died on a cross and paid the price for my sins. You must really love me a lot! You have promised in **Acts 16:31**, " *'Believe on the Lord Jesus Christ, and you will be saved.'* " I am claiming Your promise because Jesus, I do believe in You and I want to be saved. I can't wait to live with You forever in heaven. I love You with all my heart. **Amen**.

Self-Confidence

Dear Jesus, I feel that I'm just not as good as my friends and nothing that I do is good enough. Most of the time, I don't even want to try, because I know I can't do it anyway. But I found Your promise that I am claiming for myself, in **Proverbs 3:26**, *"For the LORD will be your confidence."* Please help me to be all that You want me to be so I can go forward with Your confidence. Oh, and one more thing, dear Jesus, whenever I forget, please remind me to trust in You. **Amen**.

Self-Pity

Dear Jesus, please help me not to feel sorry for myself. It seems like I don't have as much as other kids and I get all down about it and have a pity party. You have given me so much and I want to be grateful, but it's so hard! I claim Your promise in **Psalm 40:5**, *"Many, O LORD my God, are Your wonderful works which You have done; and Your thoughts toward us cannot be recounted to You in order; if I would declare and speak of them, they are more than can be numbered."* Thank You for helping me remember all the great things You do for me everyday!

Amen.

Self-Worth

Dear Jesus, I'm not feeling very good about myself right now. I've made some mistakes and people have put me down. When I get to feeling like this, I'm so thankful for Your promise in **John 15:16**, *" 'You did not choose Me, but I chose you and appointed you that you should go and bear fruit, and that your fruit should remain, that whatever you ask the Father in My name He may give you.' "* Regardless of what others might say about me, I know I am special because You have chosen me and will answer my prayers. **Amen**.

Sharing

Dear Jesus, I don't feel like sharing right now. I don't want to be selfish, but it's tough to give away something I really want. Please give me an unselfish heart. Help me to be a cheerful giver.

I claim Your promise in **Luke 6:38**, " *'Give, and it will be given to you: good measure, pressed down, shaken together, and running over will be put into your bosom [lap]. For with the same measure that you use, it will be measured back to you.'* " So Jesus I'll willingly share what I have, knowing that You will keep Your promise to give me back even more. **Amen**.

Sharing Jesus

Dear Jesus, I love You and I want my friends and neighbors to love You too. I know I can share You by being kind and good like You are. But I would also like to tell them about You. I'm kind of scared to do this because I don't know what to say. That's why I'm claiming Your promise in **Jeremiah 33:3**, " ' "Call to Me, and I will answer you, and show you great and mighty things, which you do not know." ' " Thank You Jesus for promising to give me "great and mighty" answers so I can be a better witness for You. **Amen**.

Shy

Dear Jesus, I don't know why, but I get so shy around other kids. I'm afraid I don't look good enough, or I'll say dumb things. Even though I'd like to have friends, I just clam up and feel sorry for myself. Help me to be more confident. I'm claiming **Matthew 7:7**, *"'Ask, and it will be given to you; seek, and you will find; knock, and it will be opened to you.'"* **Please help** me not to be scared and shy around others. When I'm tempted to hang back, help me to picture You beside me holding my hand so I won't have to be shy. **Amen**.

Sickness—Self

Dear Jesus, I'm sick and I just don't seem to be getting well. You healed so many people when You were here on this earth, and I know You can heal me too if it is Your will. I'm claiming Your promise in **2 Kings 20:5**, *" 'I have heard your prayer, I have seen your tears; surely I will heal you.' "* I'm feeling better already, just knowing that You have heard my prayer and will take care of me. Thank You Jesus. **Amen**.

Sins

Dear Jesus, I've done some pretty bad things and I am so ashamed. I know it makes You sad when I sin against You and when I do things that hurt others. Jesus, please forgive me for I am claiming Your promise in **Isaiah 43:25**, *" 'I, even I, am He who blots out your transgressions [mistakes] for My own sake; and I will not remember your sins.' "* Thank You Jesus for erasing all my sins and promising to forget them. I love You. **Amen**.

Sorry

Dear Jesus, I did something wrong that hurt someone. I guess I just wanted my friends to think I was cool. But it was wrong and I'm really sorry. I know I should ask for forgiveness, but I'm too embarrassed. Jesus, forgive me and give me the courage to apologize and make it right. I claim Your promise in **Ezekiel 36:26**, " *'I will give you a new heart and put a new spirit within you.'* " Thank You for forgiving me and giving me a new heart and a new spirit. I really need that. **Amen**.

Stealing

Dear Jesus, I took something that didn't belong to me and I'm feeling guilty. I know I shouldn't steal, because that's one of Your commandments. Please forgive me for stealing, give me courage to make it right, and help me not to do it again. I am claiming Your promise in **2 Chronicles 7:14**, " *'If My people who are called by My name will humble themselves, and pray and seek My face, and turn from their wicked ways, then I will hear from heaven, and will forgive their sin and heal their land.'* "

Whenever I am tempted to steal, please help me remember that stealing is a sin and give me the strength I need to obey You. **Amen.**

Strength

Dear Jesus, I don't feel very strong and I could really use Your help. I have a lot of stuff happening in my life right now and I need You just to keep going. Please give me the power and strength You promise in **Isaiah 40:29**, *"He gives power to the weak, and to those who have no might He increases strength."* Thank You for always being there for me and giving me Your strength and power to deal with all my problems! I know that I can always count on You. **Amen**.

Stress

Dear Jesus, You know what's happening in my life right now and I just can't deal with it all. I'm worried about everything! I'm basically stressed out! I don't want to let everybody down, but it's just too much. Lord, please help me! I'm claiming Your promise in **Psalm 55:22**, *"Cast your burden on the LORD, and He shall sustain you; He shall never permit the righteous to be moved [made to slip, fall, or fail]."* **Thank You** for Your promise and for taking this stress away. **Amen**.

Success

Dear Jesus, I want to be successful in everything I do. Help me to work hard and do my part, so that I can always do my best. When I make mistakes, please give me the courage to try harder the next time. I claim Your promise in **Psalm 37:4**, *"Delight yourself also in the Lord, and He shall give you the desires of your heart."* Jesus, you know what I really want in life—and what would be good for me. My desire is to live my life for You and then I know I'll be successful. Thank You Jesus. **Amen**.

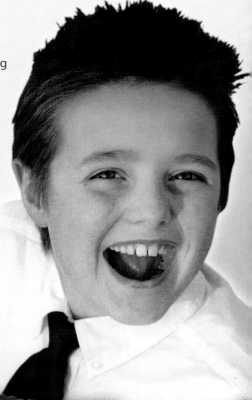

Talents

Dear Jesus, thank You for the talents You have given me. Please keep me humble and help me to remember that every talent I have comes from You. I want to use my talents to serve others. I want to always honor You. I claim Your promise in **Philippians 1:6**, *"Being confident of this very thing, that He who has begun a good work in you will complete it until the day of Jesus Christ."* Thank You for the good work You started in me. I know I'm not perfect, but with You guiding me each step of the way, I can become everything You want me to be. **Amen**.

Teasing

Dear Jesus, I got teased again today and felt like crying. I wanted to get back at them. But then I thought about You and even when people treated You mean, You were always kind. I want to be like You. I'm claiming the promise in **Hebrews 13:6**, *" 'The LORD is my helper; I will not fear. What can man [kids] do to me?' "* Please help me to forgive them, and thank You for promising to help me. I'm so glad I don't have to be afraid any more. **Amen**.

Tempted

Dear Jesus, I know what I should do, but I keep making bad decisions. Every time I fall, I say I won't do it again, but I do! I need help Lord because I really, really want to be good. So I'm claiming **Psalm 37:23, 24**, *"The steps of a good man [kid] are ordered by the LORD, and He delights in his way. Though he fall, he shall not be utterly cast down; for the LORD upholds him with His hand."* Hold on to my hand and don't let go. Pull me back up when I start to fall and give me courage to say, "Get behind me, Satan," just like You did. **Amen**.

Thankfulness

Dear Jesus, You are so good to me and have given me so much that I just want to say Thank You! It seems that I'm always asking You for stuff, but help me remember to thank You more! I especially want to thank You for Your promise of peace in **Philippians 4:6, 7,** *"Be anxious for nothing, but in everything by prayer and supplication, with thanksgiving, let your requests be made known to God; and the peace of God, which surpasses all understanding, will guard your hearts and minds through Christ Jesus."* Thank You Jesus for being such an awesome God! **Amen**.

Things I Want

Dear Jesus, there is something that I want, but I don't have enough money to buy it. I realize I'm asking a lot, but I really, really want it! I don't want to be selfish and I know You love me so much You only want me to have things that are good for me. That's why I claim Your promise in **1 John 5:14**, *"If we ask anything according to His will, He hears us."* Jesus, if this is Your will for me, please make it possible. But if not, help me to have a good attitude and not be disappointed. Thank You Jesus for always hearing my prayer. **Amen**.

Thoughts

Dear Jesus, I have trouble controlling my thoughts. I hear and see so much bad stuff that if I'm not careful, it's all I think about. But I want to be more like You, and I don't want to think sinful thoughts. That's why I'm claiming Your promise in **Romans 12:2**, *"And do not be conformed to this world, but be transformed by the renewing of your mind, that you may prove what is that good and acceptable and perfect will of God."* Please dear Jesus, renew my mind and help me to only think about good things that will bring me closer to You. **Amen**.

Time

Dear Jesus, please help me spend my time like You want me to. I do things I really don't need to do, and then I don't have time to do what I should. I'm always trying to get caught up and some days, I don't even have time to study my Bible! I want to change. I claim Your promise in **Ecclesiastes 3:1**, *"To everything there is a season, a time for every purpose under heaven."* Lord, I know I don't need more time, I just need to make better choices about how I use my time. Help me to remember that time is a valuable gift from You. Please help me use it wisely. **Amen**.

Tithe

Dear Jesus, I know I'm just a kid, but I want to do everything that You want me to do. That's why I've started giving tithe. I know it isn't much, but I want to be faithful. When I'm tempted to steal from You and keep Your money, help me remember Your promise in **Malachi 3:10**,

" 'Bring all the tithes into the storehouse, that there may be food in My house, and try Me now in this,' says the LORD of hosts, 'If I will not open for you the windows of heaven and pour out for you such blessing that there will not be room enough to receive it.' "

I'm excited about receiving Your blessings. **Amen**.

Trouble

Dear Jesus, I think I'm in trouble. I don't know what's going to happen. And I don't know what to do. I need You to soften hearts, change minds, give me the words I should say, and help me to accept whatever punishment I'm given. Most of all, I'm claiming Your promise in **Isaiah 60:10**, " *'For in My wrath I struck you, but in My favor I have had mercy on you.'* " Lord, please have mercy on me and help me to learn the lessons You want me to learn from this, so I don't have to go through this kind of trouble again. Thank You for saving me. **Amen.**

Truth

Dear Jesus, I'm confused about some of the things I read in the Bible. Some people explain it one way, and some another. But I want to know the truth. That's why I'm claiming Your promise in **John 8:31**, **32**, *" 'If you abide in My word . . . you shall know the truth, and the truth shall make you free.' "* OK, Lord. I'll do what You say. I'll keep studying Your Word. But I'm not smart enough to figure everything out. So please send the Holy Spirit to impress me with the truth. **Amen**.

TV and Video Games

Dear Jesus, help me to stop looking at things on TV that are bad for me and playing video games where I see evil things. It makes me think of Satan instead of You so I know I shouldn't do it. I claim Your promise in Isaiah **33:15** and **16**, *"He who . . . stops his ears from hearing of bloodshed, and shuts his eyes from seeing evil: he will dwell on high."* That's what I really want to do, dwell on high in heaven with You. Help me to say No to hearing and watching evil things. Help me to be the kind of kid You want me to be. **Amen**.

Vandalism

Dear Jesus, I know it's wrong—and I know I shouldn't have done it, but I went along with my friends and destroyed property. I'm so sorry and I'm ashamed of what I've done. I've asked forgiveness, I'm going to pay for the damage, and I promise to never do it again. In **Proverbs 17:13**, You say, *"Whoever rewards evil for good, evil will not depart from his house."* Lord, please save me. I don't want evil in my house! Help me to choose friends who love You and will be a better influence on me. And help me to always stand up for You and do what is right. **Amen**.

Winning

Dear Jesus, I like to win. I like to get prizes, blue ribbons, and trophies. But when I win, someone else must lose. So help me to be both a humble winner and a good loser. I know You love giving me good things, so I claim Your promise in **Matthew 7:11**, " *'If you then, being evil, know how to give good gifts to your children, how much more will your Father who is in heaven give good things to those who ask Him!'* " So Lord right now I'm asking that You'll help me win. I promise to do my best, but I trust You to decide if winning is good for me or not. And whatever happens, I'll give You the glory. **Amen**.

Words

Dear Jesus, it seems I'm always saying things that get me into trouble.
I don't like it when people say hurtful things to me.
And I know I've hurt my family and my friends by
some of the things I've said. I'm so sorry.
Please forgive me and help me remember to
control my tongue as I claim **Proverbs 18:21**,
"Death and life are in the power of the
tongue, and those who love it [indulge it]
will eat its fruit [death or life]." Lord, please
help me to think before I speak, and even
if I'm mad, help me only to say
kind things. **Amen**.

Worry

Dear Jesus, I worry about so many things. It seems I worry about almost everything! I know it doesn't help to worry, but these things just go around and around in my mind. Jesus, please give me more faith in You and take away my worries. In their place I claim Your promise in **Romans 8:28**, *"And we know that all things work together for good to those who love God, to those who are the called according to His purpose."* Help me to worry less and trust You more, knowing that You'll work everything out! Thank You for Your promise. **Amen**.

Worship

Dear Jesus, You have done so much for me and I want to show You how much I love You. The truth is, I don't even really know how to worship You like I should. Please show me how to give You praise and honor. In **1 Chronicles 16:29**, You say, *"Give to the LORD the glory due His name; . . . come before Him. Oh, worship the LORD."* Please help me to give You glory and worship You more. You are such an awesome God and I want to honor You. Help me to be quiet and respectful in church and to speak Your name with reverence and respect. **Amen.**

Bible Promises Used in This Book

Exodus 4:12, *" 'I will be with your mouth and teach you what you shall say.' "* **(Arguing)**

Deuteronomy 20:4, *" ' "For the LORD your God is He who goes with you, to fight for you against your enemies, to save you." ' "* **(Rejection)**

Deuteronomy 28:13, *" 'And the LORD will make you the head and not the tail; you shall be above only, and not be beneath, if you heed the commandments of the LORD your God, which I command you today, and are careful to observe them.' "* **(Leader)**

1 Samuel 12:23, *" 'I will teach you the good and the right way.' "* **(Fighting)**

2 Kings 20:5, *" 'I have heard your prayer, I have seen your tears; surely I will heal you.' "* **(Sickness—Self)**

1 Chronicles 16:29, *"Give to the LORD the glory due His name; . . . come before Him. Oh, worship the LORD."* **(Worship)**

2 Chronicles 7:14, *" 'If My people who are called by My name will humble themselves, and pray and seek My face, and turn from their wicked ways, then I will hear from heaven, and will forgive their sin and heal their land.' "* **(Stealing)**

2 Chronicles 16:9, *" 'For the eyes of the LORD run to and fro throughout the whole earth, to show Himself strong on behalf of those whose heart is loyal to Him.' "* **(Loyalty)**

Job 5:21, *" 'You shall be hidden from the scourge of the tongue.' "* **(Gossiping)**

Psalm 22:19, *"But You, O LORD, do not be far from Me; O My Strength, hasten to help Me!"* **(Embarrassed)**

Psalm 30:2, *"O LORD my God, I cried out to You, and You healed me."* **(Pets—Sick)**

Psalm 31:24, *"Be of good courage, and He shall strengthen your heart, all you who hope in the LORD."* **(Courage)**

Psalm 32:2, *"Blessed is the man [kid] . . . in whose spirit there is no deceit."* **(Honesty)**

Psalm 32:8, *"I will instruct you and teach you in the way you should go; I will guide you with My eye."* **(Learning)**

Psalm 34:7, *"The angel of the LORD encamps all around those who fear Him, and delivers them."* **(Afraid of the Dark)**

Psalm 34:10, *"But those that seek the LORD shall not lack any good thing."* **(Money)**

Psalm 34:18, *"The LORD is near to those who have a broken heart, and saves such as have a contrite [humble] spirit."* **(Divorce of Parents)**

Psalm 37:4, *"Delight yourself also in the LORD, and He shall give you the desires of your heart."* **(Success)**

Psalm 37:23, 24, *"The steps of a good man [kid] are ordered by the LORD, and He delights in his way. Though he fall, he shall not be utterly cast down; for the LORD upholds him with His hand."* **(Tempted)**

Psalm 37:34, *"Wait on the LORD, and keep His way, and He shall exalt you to inherit the land."* **(Patience)**

Psalm 38:15, *"For in You, O LORD, I hope; You will hear, O Lord my God."* **(Hope)**

Psalm 40:5, *"Many, O LORD my God, are Your wonderful works which You have done; and Your thoughts toward us cannot be recounted to You in order; if I would declare and speak of them, they are more than can be numbered."* **(Self-Pity)**

Psalm 50:23, *" 'Whoever offers praise glorifies Me; and to him who orders his conduct aright I will show the salvation of God.' "* **(Bad Temper)**

Psalm 55:22, *"Cast your burden on the LORD, and He shall sustain you; He shall never permit the righteous to be moved [made to slip, fall, or fail]."* **(Stress)**

Psalm 84:11, *"The LORD will give grace and glory; no good thing will He withhold from those who walk uprightly [do what is right]."* **(Blessings From God)**

Psalm 85:13, *"Righteousness will go before Him, and shall make His footsteps our pathway."* **(Safe Travel)**

Psalm 91:3, 4, *"Surely He shall deliver you from the snare of the fowler [hidden traps] and from the perilous pestilence [deadly diseases]. He shall cover* you with His feathers, and under His wings you shall take refuge; His truth shall be your shield and buckler [protection]." **(Protection)**

Psalm 91:11, *"For He shall give His angels charge over you, to keep you in all your ways."* **(Bedtime Prayer)**

Psalm 91:15, *"He shall call upon Me, and I will answer him; I will be with him in trouble; I will deliver him and honor him."* **(Failure)**

Psalm 103:2–4, "Bless the LORD, O my soul, and forget not all His benefits: who forgives all your iniquities, who heals all your diseases, who redeems your life from destruction, who crowns you with lovingkindness and tender mercies." **(Praising God)**

Psalm 119:11, *"Your word I have hidden in my heart, that I might not sin against You."* **(Bible Study)**

Proverbs 3:24, *"When you lie down, you will not be afraid; yes, you will lie down and your sleep will be sweet."* **(Afraid to Sleep)**

Proverbs 3:26, *"For the LORD will be your confidence."* **(Self-Confidence)**

Proverbs 12:25, *"Anxiety in the heart of man [kids] causes depression, but a good word makes it glad."* **(Complaining)**

Proverbs 12:28, *"In the way of righteousness [doing right] is life."* **(Kindness)**

Proverbs 13:18, *"Poverty and shame will come to him who distains correction, but he who regards a rebuke will be honored."* **(Punishment)**

Proverbs 14:30, *"A sound [calm] heart is life to the body, but envy [jealousy] is rottenness to the bones."* **(Jealousy)**

Proverbs 15:8, *"The sacrifice of the wicked is an abomination to the LORD, but the prayer of the upright is His delight."* **(Prayer)**

Proverbs 16:7, *"When a man's [kid's] ways please the LORD, He makes even his enemies to be at peace with him."* **(Bad Sport)**

Proverbs 16:20, *"Whoever trusts in the LORD, happy is he."* **(Happiness)**

Proverbs 16:32, *"He who is slow to anger is better than the mighty, and he who rules his spirit than he who takes a city."* **(Anger)**

Proverbs 17:13, *"Whoever rewards evil for good, evil will not depart from his house."* (Vandalism)

Proverbs 18:21, *"Death and life are in the power of the tongue, and those who love it [indulge it] will eat its fruit [death or life]."* (Words)

Proverbs 22:29, *"Do you see a man [kid] who excels in his work? He will stand before kings; he will not stand before unknown men."* (Homework)

Proverbs 27:21, *"The refining pot is for silver and the furnace for gold, and a man is valued by what others say of him."* (Reputation)

Proverbs 28:19, *"He who tills his land will have plenty of bread, but he who follows frivolity [wastes time] will have poverty enough!"* (Lazy)

Ecclesiastes 3:1, *"To everything there is a season, a time for every purpose under heaven."* (Time)

Isaiah 30:18, *"For the Lord is a God of justice; blessed are all those who wait for Him."* (Fairness)

Isaiah 33:15, 16, *"He who . . . stops his ears from hearing of bloodshed, and shuts his eyes from seeing evil: he will dwell on high."* (TV and Video Games)

Isaiah 40:29, *"He gives power to the weak, and to those who have no might He increases strength."* (Strength)

Isaiah 41:10, *" ' "Fear not, for I am with you; be not dismayed, for I am your God. I will strengthen you, yes, I will help you, I will uphold you with My righteous right hand." ' "* (Afraid of Bullies)

Isaiah 43:25, *" 'I, even I, am He who blots out your transgressions [mistakes] for My own sake; and I will not remember your sins.' "* (Sins)

Isaiah 46:11, *" 'I have spoken it; I will also bring it to pass.' "* (Doubt)

Isaiah 54:10, *" 'For the mountains shall depart and the hills be removed, but My kindness shall not depart from you.' "* (Friendship With Jesus)

Isaiah 56:2, *" 'Blessed is the man [kid] . . . who keeps from defiling the Sabbath,' and keeps his hand from doing any evil.' "* (Sabbath)

Isaiah 60:10, *" 'For in My wrath I struck you, but in My favor I have had mercy on you.' "* (Trouble)

Jeremiah 29:11, *"For I know the thoughts [and plans] that I think toward you, says the Lord,* *thoughts of peace and not of evil, to give you a future and a hope."* (**Good Morning Prayer**)

Jeremiah 30:17, *" ' "For I will restore health to you and heal you of your wounds." ' "* (**Healing**)

Jeremiah 31:13, *" 'For I will turn their mourning to joy, will comfort them, and make them rejoice rather than sorrow.' "* (**Comfort**)

Jeremiah 33:3, *" ' "Call to Me, and I will answer you, and show you great and mighty things, which you do not know." ' "* (**Sharing Jesus**)

Ezekiel 36:26, *" 'I will give you a new heart and put a new spirit within you.' "* (**Sorry**)

Malachi 3:10, *" 'Bring all the tithes into the storehouse, that there may be food in my house. . and try Me now in this,' says the LORD of hosts, 'If I will not open for you the windows of heaven and pour out for you such blessing that such there will not be room enough to receive it.' "* (**Tithe**)

Matthew 5:11, 12, *" 'Blessed are you when they revile and persecute you, and say all kinds of evil against you falsely.' "* (**Falsely Accused**)

Matthew 6:8, *" 'For your Father knows the things you have need of before you ask Him.' "* (**Confused**)

Matthew 6:25, *" 'Do not worry about your life, what you will eat or what you will drink.' "* (**Blessing for Meals**)

Matthew 7:7, *" 'Ask, and it will be given to you; seek, and you will find; knock, and it will be opened to you.' "* (**Shy**)

Matthew 7:11, *" 'If you then, being evil, know how to give good gifts to your children, how much more will your Father who is in heaven give good things to those who ask Him!' "* (**Winning**)

Matthew 17:20, *" 'If you have faith as a mustard seed, you will say to this mountain, "Move from here to there," and it will move; and nothing will be impossible for you.' "* (**Lost Object**)

Matthew 21:22, *" 'And whatever things you ask in prayer, believing, you will receive.' "* (**Faith**)

Mark 10:27, *" 'With men [kids] it is impossible, but not with God; for with God all things are possible.' "* (**Lying**)

Mark 13:31, *" 'Heaven and earth will pass away, but My words will by no means pass away.' "* (**Bible Truth**)

Luke 6:35, " 'But love your enemies, do good . . . and your reward will be great, and you will be sons of the Most High. For He is kind to the unthankful and evil.' " (Criticism)

Luke 6:37, " 'Forgive, and you will be forgiven.' " (Forgiving Others)

Luke 6:38, " 'Give, and it will be given to you: good measure, pressed down, shaken together, and running over will be put into your bosom [lap]. For with the same measure that you use, it will be measured back to you.' " (Sharing)

Luke 14:11, " 'For whoever exalts himself will be humbled, and he who humbles himself will be exalted.' " (Pride)

John 3:16, " 'For God so loved the world that He gave His only begotten Son, that whoever believes in Him should not perish but have everlasting life.' " (Heaven)

John 8:31, 32, " 'If you abide in My word . . . you shall know the truth, and the truth shall make you free.' " (Truth)

John 11:22, " 'But even now I know that whatever You ask of God, God will give You.' " (Eating Disorders)

John 13:17, " 'If you know these things, blessed [happy] are you if you do them.' " (Rules)

John 14:2, 3, " 'In My Father's house are many mansions; if it were not so, I would have told you. I go to prepare a place for you. And if I go and prepare a place for you, I will come again and receive you to Myself; that where I am, there you may be also.' " (Living With Jesus)

John 14:14, " 'If you ask anything in My name, I will do it.' " (Friends—Choosing the Right Ones)

John 14:27, " 'Peace I leave with you, My peace I give to you; not as the world gives do I give to you. Let not your heart be troubled, neither let it be afraid.' " (Afraid to be Alone)

John 15:16, " 'You did not choose Me, but I chose you and appointed you that you should go and bear fruit, and that your fruit should remain, that whatever you ask the Father in My name He may give you.' " (Self-Worth)

John 16:23, "Most assuredly, I say to you, whatever you ask the Father in My name, He will give you.' " (Pets—Lost)

John 16:24, " 'Ask, and you will receive, that your

joy may be full.' " (Attitude)

Acts 16:31, " 'Believe on the Lord Jesus Christ, and you will be saved.' " (Saved)

Romans 8:28, *"And we know that all things work together for good to those that love God, to those who are the called according to His purpose."* (Worry)

Romans 12:2, *"And do not be conformed to this world, but be transformed by the renewing of your mind, that you may prove what is that good and acceptable and perfect will of God."* (Thoughts)

Romans 15:7, *"Therefore receive [accept] one another, just as Christ also received [accepted] us, to the glory of God."* (Accepting Others)

2 Corinthians 5:17, *"Therefore, if anyone is in Christ, he is a new creation; old things have passed away; behold all things have become new."* (Changing Behavior)

Galatians 6:4, 5, *"But let each one examine his own work, and then he will have rejoicing in himself alone, and not in another. For each one shall bear his own load."* (Comparing)

Galatians 6:7, *"Whatever a man [kid] sows, that he will also reap."* (Friends—Making Friends)

Galatians 6:9, *"Let us not grow weary while doing good, for in due season we shall reap if we do not lose heart."* (Discouraged)

Ephesians 2:8, 9, *"For by grace you have been saved through faith, and that not of yourselves; it is the gift of God, not of works, lest anyone should boast."* (Bragging)

Ephesians 5:2, *"And walk in love, [esteeming and delighting in one another] as Christ also has loved us and given Himself for us, an offering and a sacrifice to God for a sweet-smelling aroma."* (Family)

Ephesians 6:1–3, *"Children, obey your parents in the Lord, for this is right. 'Honor your father and mother,' which is the first commandment with promise: 'that it may be well with you and you may live long on the earth.' "* (Obeying Parents)

Philippians 1:6, *"Being confident of this very thing, that He who has begun a good work in you will complete it until the day of Jesus Christ."* (Talents)

Philippians 4:6, 7, *"Be anxious for nothing, but in everything by prayer and supplication, with thanksgiving, let your requests be made known to God; and the peace of God, which surpasses all understanding, will guard your hearts and minds through Christ Jesus."* **(Thankfulness)**

Philippians 4:13, *"I can do all things through Christ who strengthens me."* **(Bad Habits)**

Philippians 4:19, *"And my God shall supply all your need."* **(Cheating)**

1 Thessalonians 4:16, 17, *"And the dead in Christ will rise first. Then we who are alive and remain shall be caught up together with them in the clouds to meet the Lord in the air. And thus we shall always be with the Lord."* **(Afraid of Dying)**

2 Thessalonians 3:3, *"But the Lord is faithful, who will establish you and guard you from the evil one."* **(Afraid of the Devil)**

Hebrews 13:5, *" 'I will never leave you nor forsake you.' "* **(Lonely)**

Hebrews 13:6, *" 'The LORD is my helper; I will not fear. What can man [kids] do to me?' "* **(Teasing)**

James 1:5, *"If any of you lacks wisdom, let him ask of God, who gives to all liberally and without reproach, and it will be given to him."* **(Choices)**

James 4:7, *"Resist the devil and he will flee from you."* **(Rebellion)**

1 John 1:9, *"If we confess our sins, He is faithful and just to forgive us our sins and to cleanse us from all unrighteousness."* **(Guilty Feelings)**

1 John 4:12, *"If we love one another, God abides in us, and His love has been perfected in us."* **(Love)**

1 John 5:14, *"If we ask anything according to His will, He hears us."* **(Things I Want)**

1 John 5:15, *"That . . . whatever we ask, we know that we have the petitions that we have asked of Him."* **(Overeating)**